BELONGS TO:

> " A CLEAR VISION, BACKED BY DEFINITE PLANS, GIVES YOU A TREMENDOUS FEELING OF CONFIDENCE AND PERSONAL POWER. "
> ~ BRIAN TRACY

FIVE-YEAR GOALS

FROM: _____ TO: _____

ONE-YEAR GOALS

FOR: _____

》 WHAT IS MY „WHY" 《

FIVE-YEAR PLAN 1st YEAR _____

FIVE-YEAR PLAN 2nd YEAR _____

Five-Year Plan 3rd Year _____

Five-Year Plan 4rd Year _____

Five-Year Plan 5th Year _____

One-Year Goals By Category

Categories	Family	Friends	Health	Sport	Education	Love
January						
February						
March						
April						
May						
June						
July						
August						
September						
October						
November						
December						

One-Year Goals By Category

Categories	Finance	Business	Career	Recreation	Enviroment	For Others
January						
February						
March						
April						
May						
June						
July						
August						
September						
October						
November						
December						

The Way To achieve My Goals In _____ Year

JANUARY

FEBRUARY

MARCH

APRIL

MAY

JUNE

The Way To achieve My Goals In _____ Year

JULY

AUGUST

SEPTEMBER

OCTOBER

NOVEMBER

DECEMBER

> "A Person Who Never Made A Mistake Never Tried Anything New"
>
> - Albert Einstein

Goals For This Week

- [ ] _____
- [ ] _____
- [ ] _____
- [ ] _____
- [ ] _____

Monday __/__/____

Tuesday __/__/____

Wednesday __/__/____

Thursday __/__/____

Friday __/__/____

Saturday __/__/____

Sunday __/__/____

Success Of This Week

> "Be Happy With What You Have, While Working For What You Want"
>
> – Helen Keller

Goals For This Week

- [ ]
- [ ]
- [ ]
- [ ]
- [ ]

Monday __/__/____

Tuesday __/__/____

Wednesday __/__/____

| THURSDAY __/__/____ | FRIDAY __/__/____ |

| SATURDAY __/__/____ | SUNDAY __/__/____ |

SUCCESS OF THIS WEEK

"Believe You Can And Your Are Halfway There"

- Theodore Roosevelt

Goals For This Week

| Monday __/__/___ |

| Tuesday __/__/___ | Wednesday __/__/___ |

Thursday __/__/____

Friday __/__/____

Saturday __/__/____

Sunday __/__/____

Success Of This Week

> "Choose A Job You Love, And You Will Never Have To Work A Day In Your Life"
>
> - Confucius

Goals For This Week

- [ ]
- [ ]
- [ ]
- [ ]
- [ ]

Monday __/__/___

Tuesday __/__/___

Wednesday __/__/___

| Thursday __/__/____ | Friday __/__/____ |

| Saturday __/__/____ | Sunday __/__/____ |

Success Of This Week

"Do Not Let What You Cannot Do Interfere With What You Can Do"

- John Wooden

Goals For This Week

- [ ]
- [ ]
- [ ]
- [ ]
- [ ]

Monday __/__/___

Tuesday __/__/___

Wednesday __/__/___

Thursday __/__/____	Friday __/__/____

Saturday __/__/____	Sunday __/__/____

Success Of This Week

"Don't Stunt Wirk Is Risky, But It's Something I Enjoy"

— Verne Troyer

Goals For This Week

- [ ]
- [ ]
- [ ]
- [ ]
- [ ]

Monday __/__/___

Tuesday __/__/___

Wednesday __/__/___

Thursday __/__/____

Friday __/__/____

Saturday __/__/____

Sunday __/__/____

Success Of This Week

"Don't Try Be Oryginal, Just Try To Be Good"

- Paul Rand

Goals For This Week

- [ ]
- [ ]
- [ ]
- [ ]
- [ ]

Monday __/__/___

Tuesday __/__/___

Wednesday __/__/___

| Thursday __/__/____ | Friday __/__/____ |

| Saturday __/__/____ | Sunday __/__/____ |

Success Of This Week

> "Everyone's Dream Can Come True If You just Stick To It And Work Hard"
> - Serena Williams

Goals For This Week

- [ ]
- [ ]
- [ ]
- [ ]
- [ ]

Monday __/__/___

Tuesday __/__/___

Wednesday __/__/___

| THURSDAY __/__/____ | | FRIDAY __/__/____ |

| SATURDAY __/__/____ | | SUNDAY __/__/____ |

SUCCESS OF THIS WEEK

> "Facus On Being Productive Instead Of Busy"
>
> - Tim Ferris

Goals For This Week

- [ ]
- [ ]
- [ ]
- [ ]
- [ ]

Monday __/__/____

Tuesday __/__/____

Wednesday __/__/____

Thursday __/__/____

Friday __/__/____

Saturday __/__/____

Sunday __/__/____

Success Of This Week

"Find Your Passion, Set A Goal, Go To Work, Evaluate, Reassess And Repeat"
— Elana Meyers

Goals For This Week

- [ ]
- [ ]
- [ ]
- [ ]
- [ ]

Monday __/__/____

Tuesday __/__/____

Wednesday __/__/____

| Thursday __/__/____ | Friday __/__/____ |

| Saturday __/__/____ | Sunday __/__/____ |

Success Of This Week

> "Go As Far As You Can See; When You Get There, You'll Be Able To See Futher"
> — Thomas Carlyle

Goals For This Week

- [ ] _____
- [ ] _____
- [ ] _____
- [ ] _____
- [ ] _____

Monday __/__/___

Tuesday __/__/___

Wednesday __/__/___

Thursday __/__/____

Friday __/__/____

Saturday __/__/____

Sunday __/__/____

Success Of This Week

"Hard Work Always Wins In The End"

- Lucas Till

Goals For This Week

- [ ]
- [ ]
- [ ]
- [ ]
- [ ]

Monday __/__/___

Tuesday __/__/___

Wednesday __/__/___

| THURSDAY __/__/____ | FRIDAY __/__/____ |

| SATURDAY __/__/____ | SUNDAY __/__/____ |

SUCCESS OF THIS WEEK

> "I Have Not Failed. I've Just Found 10,000 Ways That Won't Work"
>
> — Thomas A. Edison

Goals For This Week

- [ ]
- [ ]
- [ ]
- [ ]
- [ ]

Monday __/__/____

Tuesday __/__/____

Wednesday __/__/____

| Thursday __/__/____ | Friday __/__/____ |

| Saturday __/__/____ | Sunday __/__/____ |

Success Of This Week

> "IF EVERYTHING SEEMS UNDER CONTROLL, YOU ARE NOT GOING FAST ENOUGHT"
>
> - MORIO ANGRETTI

GOALS FOR THIS WEEK

- [ ]
- [ ]
- [ ]
- [ ]
- [ ]

MONDAY __/__/____

TUESDAY __/__/____

WEDNESDAY __/__/____

Thursday __/__/____

Friday __/__/____

Saturday __/__/____

Sunday __/__/____

Success Of This Week

"If You Do What You Love, You Will Never Work A Day In Your Life"

— Marc Anthony

Goals For This Week

| Monday __/__/___ |

☐
☐
☐
☐
☐

| Tuesday __/__/___ | Wednesday __/__/___ |

| Thursday __/__/____ | Friday __/__/____ |

| Saturday __/__/____ | Sunday __/__/____ |

Success Of This Week

"If You Don't Build Your Own Dream, Someone Will Hire You To Build Theirs"

— Tony Haskings Jr.

Goals For This Week

- [ ] _____
- [ ] _____
- [ ] _____
- [ ] _____
- [ ] _____

Monday __/__/____

Tuesday __/__/____

Wednesday __/__/____

| THURSDAY __/__/____ | FRIDAY __/__/____ |

| SATURDAY __/__/____ | SUNDAY __/__/____ |

SUCCESS OF THIS WEEK

> "If You Really Want To Do Something. You Will Work Hard For It"
>
> — Edmund Hillary

Goals For This Week

- [ ] _____
- [ ] _____
- [ ] _____
- [ ] _____
- [ ] _____

Monday __/__/____

Tuesday __/__/____

Wednesday __/__/____

Thursday __/__/____

Friday __/__/____

Saturday __/__/____

Sunday __/__/____

Success Of This Week

> "If You See It In Your Mind, You Will Hold In Your Hand"
>
> - Bob Proctor

Goals For This Week

- [ ]
- [ ]
- [ ]
- [ ]
- [ ]

Monday __/__/___

Tuesday __/__/___

Wednesday __/__/___

Thursday __/__/____

Friday __/__/____

Saturday __/__/____

Sunday __/__/____

Success Of This Week

> "It's Important To Se Your Own Goals And Work Hard To Achieve Them"
> — Yuichiro Miura

Goals For This Week

- [ ] _____
- [ ] _____
- [ ] _____
- [ ] _____
- [ ] _____

Monday __/__/____

Tuesday __/__/____

Wednesday __/__/____

Thursday __/__/____

Friday __/__/____

Saturday __/__/____

Sunday __/__/____

Success Of This Week

> "LIFE ISN'T ABAUT FINDING YOURSELF. LIFE IS ABOUT CREATING YOURSELF"
> - GEORGE BERNARD SHAW

GOALS FOR THIS WEEK

- [ ]
- [ ]
- [ ]
- [ ]
- [ ]

MONDAY __/__/___

TUESDAY __/__/___

WEDNESDAY __/__/___

Thursday __/__/____

Friday __/__/____

Saturday __/__/____

Sunday __/__/____

Success Of This Week

"Life Isn't About Finding Yourself. Life Is About Creating Yourself"

— George B. Shaw

Goals For This Week

- [ ]
- [ ]
- [ ]
- [ ]
- [ ]

Monday __/__/___

Tuesday __/__/___

Wednesday __/__/___

| THURSDAY __/__/____ | FRIDAY __/__/____ |

| SATURDAY __/__/____ | SUNDAY __/__/____ |

SUCCESS OF THIS WEEK

"Live Is 10% Happen To Us And 90% How We React To It"

— Dennis P. Kimbro

Goals For This Week

- [ ]
- [ ]
- [ ]
- [ ]
- [ ]

Monday __/__/___

Tuesday __/__/___

Wednesday __/__/___

| THURSDAY __/__/____ | FRIDAY __/__/____ |

| SATURDAY __/__/____ | SUNDAY __/__/____ |

SUCCESS OF THIS WEEK

> "Make Every Detail Perfect And Limit The Number Of Details To Perfect"
>
> — Jack Dorsey

Goals For This Week

- [ ] _____
- [ ] _____
- [ ] _____
- [ ] _____
- [ ] _____

Monday __/__/____

Tuesday __/__/____

Wednesday __/__/____

Thursday __/__/____

Friday __/__/____

Saturday __/__/____

Sunday __/__/____

Success Of This Week

> "Make Your Life A Masterpice: Imagine No Limitations On What You Can Be Or Do"
> - Brian Tracy

Goals For This Week

- [ ]
- [ ]
- [ ]
- [ ]
- [ ]

Monday __/__/____

Tuesday __/__/____

Wednesday __/__/____

| THURSDAY __/__/____ | FRIDAY __/__/____ |

| SATURDAY __/__/____ | SUNDAY __/__/____ |

SUCCESS OF THIS WEEK

> "Never Live That Till Tomorrow Which You Can Do Today"
>
> - Benjamin Franclin

Goals For This Week

- [ ]
- [ ]
- [ ]
- [ ]
- [ ]

Monday __/__/____

Tuesday __/__/____

Wednesday __/__/____

Thursday __/__/____

Friday __/__/____

Saturday __/__/____

Sunday __/__/____

Success Of This Week

> "Nothing In Life Is To Be Feared, It Is Only To Be Understood"
>
> - Maria Curie

Goals For This Week

- [ ]
- [ ]
- [ ]
- [ ]
- [ ]

Monday ___/___/____

Tuesday ___/___/____

Wednesday ___/___/____

| Thursday __/__/____ | | Friday __/__/____ |

| Saturday __/__/____ | | Sunday __/__/____ |

Success Of This Week

> "Peopl Who Say It Cannot Be Done Should Not Interrupt Those Who Are Doing It"
> — George Bernard

Goals For This Week

- [ ] _____
- [ ] _____
- [ ] _____
- [ ] _____
- [ ] _____

Monday __/__/____

Tuesday __/__/____

Wednesday __/__/____

Thursday __/__/____

Friday __/__/____

Saturday __/__/____

Sunday __/__/____

Success Of This Week

> "Plann Your Work For Today And Every Day. Then Work Your Plan"
>
> - Margaret Thatcher

Goals For This Week

- [ ] _____
- [ ] _____
- [ ] _____
- [ ] _____
- [ ] _____

Monday __/__/____

Tuesday __/__/____

Wednesday __/__/____

| Thursday __/__/____ | Friday __/__/____ |

| Saturday __/__/____ | Sunday __/__/____ |

👏 Success Of This Week

> "Possitive Thinking Will Let You Do Everything Better Than Negative Thinking Will"
> — Zig Ziglar

Goals For This Week

- [ ]
- [ ]
- [ ]
- [ ]
- [ ]

Monday __/__/___

Tuesday __/__/___

Wednesday __/__/___

| Thursday __/__/____ | Friday __/__/____ |

| Saturday __/__/____ | Sunday __/__/____ |

Success Of This Week

> "Self-Disciplie Is What Separates The Winners And The Losers"
>
> \- Thomas Peterffy

Goals For This Week

- [ ] _____
- [ ] _____
- [ ] _____
- [ ] _____
- [ ] _____

Monday __/__/____

Tuesday __/__/____

Wednesday __/__/____

Thursday __/__/____

Friday __/__/____

Saturday __/__/____

Sunday __/__/____

Success Of This Week

> "Set You Goals High, And Don't Stop Till You Get There"
>
> — Bo Jacson

Goals For This Week

- [ ]
- [ ]
- [ ]
- [ ]
- [ ]

Monday __/__/___

Tuesday __/__/___

Wednesday __/__/___

Thursday __/__/____

Friday __/__/____

Saturday __/__/____

Sunday __/__/____

Success Of This Week

> "Since Everything Is In Our Heads, We Had Better Not Lose Them"
>
> - Coco Chanel

Goals For This Week

- [ ]
- [ ]
- [ ]
- [ ]
- [ ]

Monday __/__/____

Tuesday __/__/____

Wednesday __/__/____

| Thursday __/__/____ | Friday __/__/____ |

| Saturday __/__/____ | Sunday __/__/____ |

Success Of This Week

> "Some People Dream Of Success While Others Wake Up And Work Hard At It"
>
> - Napoleon Hill

Goals For This Week

- [ ]
- [ ]
- [ ]
- [ ]
- [ ]

Monday __/__/____

Tuesday __/__/____

Wednesday __/__/____

Thursday __/__/____

Friday __/__/____

Saturday __/__/____

Sunday __/__/____

Success Of This Week

> "Success Is Consequence And Must Not Be A Goal"
> — Gustave Flaubert

Goals For This Week

- [ ]
- [ ]
- [ ]
- [ ]
- [ ]

Monday __/__/____

Tuesday __/__/____

Wednesday __/__/____

Thursday __/__/____

Friday __/__/____

Saturday __/__/____

Sunday __/__/____

Success Of This Week

> "Success Is Not Final, Failure Is Not Fatal"
>
> - Winston Churchill

Goals For This Week

- [ ]
- [ ]
- [ ]
- [ ]
- [ ]

Monday __/__/___

Tuesday __/__/___

Wednesday __/__/___

| Thursday __/__/____ | Friday __/__/____ |

| Saturday __/__/____ | Sunday __/__/____ |

Success Of This Week

"Success Is That Old ABC" Ability, Breaks And Courage"

— Charles Luckman

Goals For This Week

- [ ]
- [ ]
- [ ]
- [ ]
- [ ]

Monday __/__/____

Tuesday __/__/____

Wednesday __/__/____

| Thursday __/__/____ | Friday __/__/____ |

| Saturday __/__/____ | Sunday __/__/____ |

Success Of This Week

"Success Is The Sum Of Small Efforts, Repeated Day In And Day Out"

— Robert Collier

Goals For This Week

- [ ]
- [ ]
- [ ]
- [ ]
- [ ]

Monday __/__/____

Tuesday __/__/____

Wednesday __/__/____

Thursday __/__/____

Friday __/__/____

Saturday __/__/____

Sunday __/__/____

Success Of This Week

> "Success People Do What Unsuccessful People Are Not Willing To Do"
>
> - Jim Rohn

Goals For This Week

Monday __/__/___

- [ ]
- [ ]
- [ ]
- [ ]
- [ ]

Tuesday __/__/___

Wednesday __/__/___

Thursday __/__/____

Friday __/__/____

Saturday __/__/____

Sunday __/__/____

Success Of This Week

> "Tell me, what is you plan to do with your wild and precious life?"
>
> — Mary Oliwer

Goals For This Week

- [ ] _____
- [ ] _____
- [ ] _____
- [ ] _____
- [ ] _____

Monday __/__/____

Tuesday __/__/____

Wednesday __/__/____

Thursday __/__/____

Friday __/__/____

Saturday __/__/____

Sunday __/__/____

Success Of This Week

"The Furure Dends On What You Do Today"

- Mahatma Gandhi

Goals For This Week

☐
☐
☐
☐
☐

Monday __/__/____

Tuesday __/__/____

Wednesday __/__/____

Thursday __/__/____

Friday __/__/____

Saturday __/__/____

Sunday __/__/____

Success Of This Week

> "The Journey Is What Brings Us Happiness, Not The Destination"
>
> - Dan Millman

Goals For This Week

- [ ]
- [ ]
- [ ]
- [ ]
- [ ]

Monday __/__/____

Tuesday __/__/____

Wednesday __/__/____

| Thursday __/__/____ | Friday __/__/____ |

| Saturday __/__/____ | Sunday __/__/____ |

Success Of This Week

> "The Most Successful People Are Those Who Are Good At Plan B"
>
> - James Yorke

Goals For This Week

- [ ]
- [ ]
- [ ]
- [ ]
- [ ]

Monday __/__/____

Tuesday __/__/____

Wednesday __/__/____

| THURSDAY __/__/____ | FRIDAY __/__/____ |

| SATURDAY __/__/____ | SUNDAY __/__/____ |

SUCCESS OF THIS WEEK

> "The Only Way To Do Great Work Is To Love What You Do"
>
> - Steve Jobs

Goals For This Week

- [ ]
- [ ]
- [ ]
- [ ]
- [ ]

Monday __/__/____

Tuesday __/__/____

Wednesday __/__/____

| Thursday __/__/____ | | Friday __/__/____ |

| Saturday __/__/____ | | Sunday __/__/____ |

👏 Success Of This Week

> "The Reward For Work Well Done Is The Opportunity To Do More"
>
> - Jonas Salk

Goals For This Week

- [ ]
- [ ]
- [ ]
- [ ]
- [ ]

Monday __/__/____

Tuesday __/__/____

Wednesday __/__/____

Thursday __/__/____

Friday __/__/____

Saturday __/__/____

Sunday __/__/____

Success Of This Week

> "The Road To Success And The Road To Failure Are Almost Exactly The Same"
>
> - Colin R. Davis

Goals For This Week

- [ ] _____
- [ ] _____
- [ ] _____
- [ ] _____
- [ ] _____

Monday __/__/____

Tuesday __/__/____

Wednesday __/__/____

Thursday __/__/____

Friday __/__/____

Saturday __/__/____

Sunday __/__/____

Success Of This Week

"The Secret Of Getting Ahead, Is Getting Started"

— Mark Twain

Goals For This Week

- [ ] _____
- [ ] _____
- [ ] _____
- [ ] _____
- [ ] _____

Monday __/__/____

Tuesday __/__/____

Wednesday __/__/____

| Thursday __/__/____ | | Friday __/__/____ |

| Saturday __/__/____ | | Sunday __/__/____ |

Success Of This Week

"The Value Of An Idea Lies In The Using Of It"

- Thomas Edison

Goals For This Week

- [ ] _____
- [ ] _____
- [ ] _____
- [ ] _____
- [ ] _____

Monday __/__/____

Tuesday __/__/____

Wednesday __/__/____

| Thursday __/__/____ | Friday __/__/____ |

| Saturday __/__/____ | Sunday __/__/____ |

Success Of This Week

> "There Is Nothing Permanent Except Change"
>
> - Heraclitus

Goals For This Week

- [ ]
- [ ]
- [ ]
- [ ]
- [ ]

Monday __/__/____

Tuesday __/__/____

Wednesday __/__/____

Thursday __/__/____

Friday __/__/____

Saturday __/__/____

Sunday __/__/____

Success Of This Week

"To Make Headway Improve Head"

- B. C. Forbes

Goals For This Week

- [ ]
- [ ]
- [ ]
- [ ]
- [ ]

Monday __/__/____

Tuesday __/__/____

Wednesday __/__/____

Thursday __/__/____

Friday __/__/____

Saturday __/__/____

Sunday __/__/____

Success Of This Week

"Tomorrow Belongs Tho The Peopl Who Prepare For It Today"
                                                                       - African Proverb

Goals For This Week

- [ ]
- [ ]
- [ ]
- [ ]
- [ ]

Monday __/__/____

Tuesday __/__/____

Wednesday __/__/____

| Thursday __/__/____ | Friday __/__/____ |

| Saturday __/__/____ | Sunday __/__/____ |

Success Of This Week

> "WE BECOME MORE SUCCESSFUL WHEN WE ARE HAPPIER AND MORE POSITIVE"
> — SHAWN ACHOR

GOALS FOR THIS WEEK

- [ ]
- [ ]
- [ ]
- [ ]
- [ ]

MONDAY __/__/____

TUESDAY __/__/____

WEDNESDAY __/__/____

| Thursday __/__/____ | Friday __/__/____ |

| Saturday __/__/____ | Sunday __/__/____ |

Success Of This Week

> "Well Done is Better Than Well Said"
>
> - Benjamin Franclin

Goals For This Week

- [ ]
- [ ]
- [ ]
- [ ]
- [ ]

Monday __/__/____

Tuesday __/__/____

Wednesday __/__/____

Thursday __/__/____

Friday __/__/____

Saturday __/__/____

Sunday __/__/____

Success Of This Week

> "Your Most Unhappy Customers Are Your Grates Source Of Learning"
> — Bill Gates

Goals For This Week

- [ ]
- [ ]
- [ ]
- [ ]
- [ ]

Monday __/__/____

Tuesday __/__/____

Wednesday __/__/____

| Thursday __/__/____ | Friday __/__/____ |

| Saturday __/__/____ | Sunday __/__/____ |

Success Of This Week

„As We Celebrate The End Of The Year,
It Is Good To Remember,
That There Is No True Ending,
But Just A New Beginning."

End-Of-The-Year Summary

I'm Proud Of myself Because :

Something I Could Make Better:

Next Year I Will:

My Signature

Made in United States
Orlando, FL
20 August 2024